TYRANNOSAURUS REX

LILIENSTERNUS

TARCHIA

BRACHIOSAURUS

VELOCIRAPTOR

NYASASAURUS PARRINGTONI

To the reader. Sometimes you can
dig for answers to discover the past.
—J.M.

All rights reserved. Published in the United States by Doubleday, an imprint of
Random House Children's Books, a division of Penguin Random House LLC, New York.

Doubleday and Hello, World! are registered trademarks and the
Doubleday colophon is a trademark of Penguin Random House LLC.

Visit us on the Web! rhcbooks.com

Educators and librarians, for a variety of teaching tools,
visit us at RHTeachersLibrarians.com

Library of Congress Cataloging-in-Publication Data is available upon request.
ISBN 978-0-593-56819-4 (trade) — ISBN 978-0-593-56820-0 (lib. bdg.) —
ISBN 978-0-593-56821-7 (ebook)

MANUFACTURED IN CHINA   10 9 8 7 6 5 4 3 2 1   First Edition

Random House Children's Books supports the First Amendment and celebrates the right to read.

HELLO, WORLD!®
KIDS' GUIDES

Exploring
DINOSAURS

Jill McDonald

Doubleday Books for Young Readers

Dinosaurs once ruled the planet!
Their fossils have been found on every continent on Earth.

* The word "dinosaur" means "terrible lizard."

These reptiles ranged in size from towering to tiny.
Some were speedy runners on two hind legs,
while others took their time, slowly grazing on all four.

Some were herbivores, which only ate plants.
Some were meat-eating carnivores.
And others were omnivores, eating everything.

Dinosaurs had a lot of special features needed to
survive for over 175 million years, including spikes,
horns, crests, feathers, claws, and armored bodies.

Let's go back in time and learn more
about these incredible creatures!

Dinosaurs lived during the **Mesozoic era**, which had three periods: **Triassic**, **Jurassic**, and **Cretaceous**.

In each of these times, Earth was a very different place. The changing climates, landscapes, plants, and animals affected how the dinosaurs lived and adapted.

* Humans never lived at the same time as dinosaurs. The first modern humans appeared around 300,000 years ago.

The Triassic period (252–201 million years ago) was hot and dry, with deserts, forests, and warm bodies of water. The North and South Poles were not cold and icy like they are today. Plant life included ferns and coniferous trees.

During this time, Earth had one large landmass, which hadn't yet split up into the separate continents we have today. Earth's first dinosaurs appeared, smaller than those that came later.

The Jurassic period (201–145 million years ago) saw more diverse life arrive, including birds, frogs, and many different dinosaurs. Earth's landmass started to split, making what we now call the Atlantic Ocean.

Earth's water created a more humid climate. More forests grew, and plants became taller. Long-necked dinosaurs appeared, such as Brachiosaurus.

The Cretaceous period (145–66 million years ago) was a time when sea levels rose and Earth's continents continued to separate, looking more like we know them today.

Many new flowers and leafy plants arrived—as did bees, which helped plants grow by spreading pollen. Dinosaurs grew to massive sizes, and species such as Tyrannosaurus rex and Triceratops arrived.

How do we know all this dinosaur information? A paleontologist is a scientist who studies the history of life on Earth by examining fossils. A fossil is the preserved remains of a once-living thing.

* Fossils aren't just bones. They can include many different remains of animal and plant life, such as footprints, teeth marks, leaves, fruit, nests, and eggs.

Paleontologists are like detectives! They work outdoors to find and dig up fossils, bringing them to scientific laboratories and museums to study them. Their discoveries allow us to learn about plants and animals that lived millions of years ago.

Which dinosaur came first?

Nyasasaurus parringtoni

may be the earliest dinosaur ever found.

This dinosaur wasn't very big. Its body was about the size of a Labrador retriever, but its tail was 5 feet (1.5 m) long.

Although Nyasasaurus parringtoni was small, it had a long neck, which would have allowed this herbivore to reach into trees for food.

Its bones were found in Tanzania in the 1930s. But it wasn't until 2012 that scientists learned that Nyasasaurus parringtoni had lived 243 million years ago. This proved that dinosaurs existed 10 to 15 million years earlier than was previously thought.

* Only an arm bone and some back and neck bones have been found from this dinosaur.

The STATS

Nyasasaurus parringtoni

Name means:
"Lake Nyasa lizard"

Time: Middle Triassic
243 million years ago

Location of fossils:
Tanzania

Maximum length:
10 feet (3 m)

Maximum weight:
135 pounds (60 kg)

Diet: Herbivore

QUESTION

If you were a paleontologist, where would you look for dinosaurs?

Compared with the massive, lumbering dinosaurs that arrived millions of years later, the Triassic dinosaurs were mostly smaller and quicker, dashing around on their two back legs.

Staurikosaurus

was one of the earliest dinosaurs. It was a small but strong predator.

With sharp, hooked claws, saw-like teeth, and a streamlined body, it could quickly attack and subdue its prey. Scientists believe its long tail helped it stay balanced while running.

* Staurikosaurus's teeth curved backward and were jagged like a steak knife, perfect for eating meat.

Plateosaurus

was one of the largest dinosaurs from the Triassic period and one of the earliest dinosaurs to grow to such a large size.

It had a stocky body, with short but powerful arms for grasping food and a long neck for reaching vegetation in trees.

* Plateosaurus is one of the best-researched dinosaurs, with more than one hundred skeletons found.

Staurikosaurus

Name means: "Southern Cross lizard"

Time: Late Triassic 227–221 million years ago

Location of fossils: Brazil

Maximum length: 7 feet (2 m)

Maximum weight: 66 pounds (30 kg)

Diet: Carnivore

Plateosaurus

Name means: "Broad lizard"

Time: Late Triassic 210 million years ago

Location of fossils: France, Germany, Switzerland

Maximum length: 16–33 feet (5–10 m)

Maximum weight: 8,800 pounds (4,000 kg)

Diet: Herbivore

QUESTION

If you were a dinosaur, would you be a carnivore, herbivore, or omnivore?

Herrerasaurus

was one of the earliest dinosaurs to have lived. Long, powerful hind legs helped it move fast. Its short arms had three curved claws for grasping and tearing. The jagged teeth of Herrerasaurus let us know it was a meat-eater.

* Coprolites are fossilized poop! The coprolites of Herrerasaurus contain bones but not plants, leading scientists to believe that it was a carnivore.

Liliensternus

was a speedy carnivore with sharp, slashing teeth, powerful back legs, and a long tail for balance. It may have had an unusual fin-like crest running along the top of its snout, which could have been used to attract a mate or scare off enemies.

— CREST

* Scientists think Liliensternus's body was covered in a short fuzz–like coat that helped it maintain its body temperature.

Earth changed during the Jurassic period.
The planet's one landmass started to split
apart, and the climate became wetter.
New conditions and life-forms affected
the next wave of dinosaurs, which grew
bigger, with more unusual body types.

* Brachiosaurus's front legs
were longer than its hind legs,
giving it a sloped look.

SPIKES—

Brachiosaurus

may have been too big and heavy to rear up
on its hind legs, but its long neck was perfect
for chomping vegetation in tall trees and
scooping up water from down below.

When it was first discovered in 1903,
Brachiosaurus was the largest dinosaur ever
found. Since then, bigger dinosaurs have been
revealed, including Dreadnoughtus, which may
have been as long as 85 feet (26 m).

* "Dreadnoughtus" means "fears nothing."

*The plates on Stegosaurus's back could grow as high as 2.5 feet (76 cm).

PLATES

Brachiosaurus

Name means: "Arm lizard"

Time: Late Jurassic
155–150 million years ago

Location of fossils:
Algeria, Portugal, Tanzania,
United States

Maximum length: 69 feet (21 m)

Maximum weight:
123,000 pounds (56,000 kg)

Diet: Herbivore

Stegosaurus

Name means: "Roof lizard"

Time: Late Jurassic
155–145 million years ago

Location of fossils:
Portugal, United States

Maximum length: 30 feet (9 m)

Maximum weight:
15,000 pounds (7,000 kg)

Diet: Herbivore

Stegosaurus is easy to recognize by its spiked tail and bony triangular plates, running along its back.

Scientists still debate what the plates were used for. It's possible they acted as armor, and they may have scared off enemies by making Stegosaurus seem bigger. Some scientists think they allowed Stegosaurus to soak up sun during the day and release heat at night, to control its body temperature.

QUESTION

Would you rather have a long neck or a spiked tail?

Apatosaurus

has had a confusing history. For over one hundred years, paleontologists thought it was the same species as Brontosaurus. Because Apatosaurus was named first, the name Brontosaurus got put aside. But as more fossils were found and studied, most paleontologists came to believe that they were two separate species.

While Apatosaurus and Brontosaurus looked similar, Apatosaurus was bigger and had a thicker and lower neck.

* Apatosaurus eggs could be as big as a basketball!

EGGS

Allosaurus

was a huge, strong, deadly meat-eater with strong, sharp claws, a wide jaw, and teeth like blades.

This dinosaur ate creatures it killed, as well as scavenging on animals it found dead.

* Allosaurus might even have eaten other Allosauruses!

Allosaurus had a horn over each eye, which could have been used in fighting, as protection, or to get the attention of a mate. The horns might even have shaded the eyes from the sun, like prehistoric sunglasses!

HORNS

The STATS

Apatosaurus

Name means: "Deceptive lizard"

Time: Late Jurassic
152–151 million years ago

Location of fossils:
United States

Maximum length: 90 feet (27 m)

Maximum weight:
78,000 pounds (35,000 kg)

Diet: Herbivore

Allosaurus

Name means: "Different lizard"

Time: Late Jurassic
155–145 million years ago

Location of fossils:
Portugal, United States

Maximum length: 35 feet (11 m)

Maximum weight:
3,300 pounds (1,500 kg)

Diet: Carnivore

QUESTION

Would you rather be a large, medium, or small dinosaur?

The Cretaceous period was the longest era of dinosaurs, lasting 79 million years, and was the last time when dinosaurs lived. It was also the most dangerous—a time of fierce, enormous creatures.

Tyrannosaurus Rex

was one of the most feared and ferocious carnivores ever. Its arms were short compared with its body, but they had sharp claws that could strike while T. rex was fighting and biting.

* T. rex's claws were 4 inches (10 cm) long and could cause deep wounds in its prey.

Because T. rex was so large, scientists believe it might have been slow when chasing prey. But its massive, muscular jaw was a chomping machine, lined with up to sixty jagged teeth. The largest T. rex tooth ever found was 12 inches (30 cm) long, the same length as a school ruler. T. rex's skull alone could grow as long as 5 feet (1.5 m)!

Triceratops

is a hard dinosaur to miss, with three horns and a large bony frill on its head. Its giant head made up about one-third of its body.

FRILL

Its horns helped it fend off predators such as Tyrannosaurus rex. Scientists still debate what the frill was for. It might have been used for protection, or possibly to show off and attract mates, like the antlers on today's deer.

This huge herbivore needed to eat a lot of plants to stay alive. It had a mouth like a beak, which was packed with up to 800 teeth, just right for tearing off large chunks of low-lying stalks and leaves.

* As Triceratops's teeth got worn down, new ones replaced them, just like sharks' teeth.

The STATS

Tyrannosaurus rex

Name means:
"Tyrant lizard king"

Time: Late Cretaceous 68–66 million years ago

Location of fossils: Canada, United States

Maximum length: 40 feet (12 m)

Maximum weight: 18,000 pounds (8,000 kg)

Diet: Carnivore

Triceratops

Name means:
"Three-horned face"

Time: Late Cretaceous 68–66 million years ago

Location of fossils: Canada, United States

Maximum length: 30 feet (9 m)

Maximum weight: 26,000 pounds (12,000 kg)

Diet: Herbivore

QUESTION

Which one of these Cretaceous creatures would you like to meet?

Deinocheirus

was a mystery for many years. Some of its bones were found in 1965, but several questions remained about this dinosaur. In 2006 and 2009, two more sets of Deinocheirus fossils were discovered, giving paleontologists more pieces to the puzzle.

The fossils show that this herbivore had a duck-like bill and jaws with no teeth. Like today's birds, it swallowed stones to help it digest the plants it ate.

* Scientists believe Deinocheirus may have had tail feathers!

Tarchia

Tarchia had a body covered in bony armor and a broad, club-like tail that could swing at predators. It didn't move fast, but thanks to its hard exterior, it was well protected.

Tarchia kept close to the ground. It had short, strong legs, allowing it to graze on low-lying plants.

BACK ARMOR

* Tarchia lived in the desert.

The STATS

Deinocheirus

Name means: "Horrible hand"

Time: Late Cretaceous
71–69 million years ago

Location of fossils:
Mongolia

Maximum length: 36 feet (11 m)

Maximum weight:
14,000 pounds (6,500 kg)

Diet: Omnivore

Tarchia

Name means: "Brainy one"

Time: Late Cretaceous
75–70 million years ago

Location of fossils:
Mongolia

Maximum length: 26 feet (8 m)

Maximum weight:
5,500 pounds (2,500 kg)

Diet: Herbivore

QUESTION

What special features would you have if you were a dinosaur?

Could dinosaurs swim?

Scientists believe that some dinosaurs could stay afloat in water if they needed to, but most were not natural swimmers.

Spinosaurus

was different. Because of its body shape, paleontologists think it may have spent its days in the water.

Like an alligator or crocodile, Spinosaurus had a long jaw, with nostrils on top of its snout, allowing it to breathe while swimming. Its sharp teeth would have been useful for chomping on slippery prey, like fish.

* Spinosaurus may have had webbed feet, like a duck's, for paddling.

SAIL

* Spinosaurus was huge—
larger than Tyrannosaurus rex!

WEBBED FEET

Spinosaurus also had shark-like features: Its spine grew upward into spikes, forming a sail along its back as high as 6 feet (2 m), which may have helped it swim. Its long, powerful, swishing tail could have moved it quickly through the water.

Spinosaurus

Name means: "Spine lizard"

Time: Late Cretaceous
99–93 million years ago

Location of fossils:
Egypt, Morocco

Maximum length: 58 feet (18 m)

Maximum weight:
46,000 pounds (21,000 kg)

Diet: Carnivore

QUESTION

What animals would you combine to make a dinosaur that could swim?

Not all dinosaurs were big. Some were as small as birds!

Light, feathered, and zippy,

Velociraptor

was about the size of a turkey—a scary turkey!
It would use its killer claws to grab its prey, then
follow up with its knife-like teeth. **Watch out!**

* "Velociraptor" means "quick thief."
Can you guess why?

Caudipteryx

was another bird-like dinosaur, with feathers
on its arms and tail and downy feathers covering
its body. Its name means "tail feather." It had
a mouth like a beak, with a few sharp teeth for
eating plants and insects.

Microraptor

was one of the smallest dinosaurs, weighing just over 2 pounds (1 kg). Its name means "tiny thief." Unlike Velociraptor and Caudipteryx,

this mini dinosaur may have been able to fly.

Scientists believe it used its four wings to soar like a glider airplane, possibly swooping down from trees to hunt its prey.

* Light on its feet, Compsognathus weighed around 7 pounds (3 kg).

Compsognathus

was a super-speedy meat-eating dinosaur about the size of a turkey. Some scientists think it could have run 40 miles (64 km) per hour. It was small but menacing, with sharp little teeth. Its name means "pretty jaw."

Why don't dinosaurs live today? What happened to them?

At the end of the Cretaceous period, dinosaurs disappeared. Scientists still debate why.

One popular theory is that a huge asteroid collided with Earth. Its impact was so large, it caused wildfires to spread. Volcanoes erupted around the same time, creating enough dust to block the sun's rays for many years. Without light and warmth, the climate changed, causing many plants and animals to die.

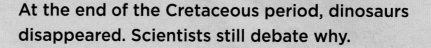

Paleontologists continue to uncover fossils, giving us further information about dinosaur species and how they lived. Many fossils are patiently pieced together and displayed in museums to share these wonders with us. Computers can now create animated images and more accurate models, which help paleontologists better understand prehistoric life.

There's so much more to discover. Perhaps one day you'll find a dinosaur too!

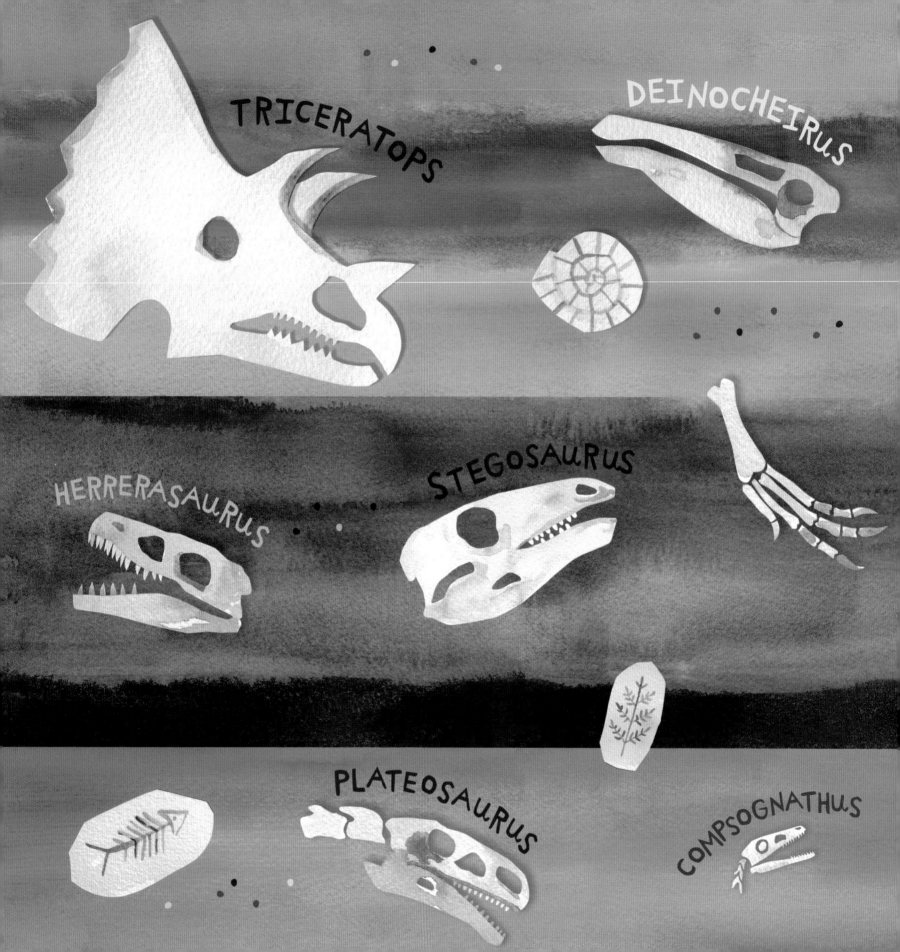

TRICERATOPS

DEINOCHEIRUS

HERRERASAURUS

STEGOSAURUS

PLATEOSAURUS

COMPSOGNATHUS